50 THINGS TO KNOW ABOUT BIRDS IN THE USA

If you know someone who loves birds, I cannot imagine them not learning or enjoying this book.

This book is perfect for both experienced birders and beginners alike. It is written in readable prose and studded with personal stories from the author's many years of observing birds.

50 Things to Know About Birds in Pennsylvania: Birding in the Keystone State
Author Darryl & Jackie Speicher

I really enjoyed this book. I live in the Badger state and I learned a lot of things I didn't know before. The author got me excited about taking up bird watching. Definitely going to plan a day trip to Horicon Marsh.

50 Things to Know About Birds in Wisconsin : Birding in the Badger State
Author Carly Lincoln

D1521455

50 THINGS TO KNOW ABOUT BIRDS IN TEXAS

Birding in the Lone Star State

Peter Palmieri

Cover designed by: Ivana Stamenkovic
Cover Image: Wikipedia

CZYK Publishing Since 2011.
CZYKPublishing.com
50 Things to Know

Lock Haven, PA
All rights reserved.
ISBN: 9798411261271

50 THINGS TO KNOW ABOUT BIRDS IN TEXAS

BOOK DESCRIPTION

Why is Texas one of the best places to see the fall migration of hawks and eagles? Where can I see roadrunners in Texas? What is the state bird of Texas? And why might that change soon? If you find yourself asking any of these questions, then this book is for you...

50 Things to Know about the Birds in Texas by Author Peter Palmieri offers an elegant approach to finding the most beautiful and varied species of birds on the continent. Most books on birding tell you to travel to specific locations and hotspots for one or two prize species on your life list. Although there's nothing wrong with that, this book takes another approach. Here we present you with the regional view of the state, and help you to locate the habitats and special locations near your travel destination. From this view, we will help you find a diverse community of birds and celebrate the similarities between species. Texas has an extraordinary geography, and there is a great overlap in breeding and wintering ranges for many species. The state is uniquely positioned to offer a variety of habitats with irruptive specialties throughout the year. Based on knowledge from the world's leading experts, understanding the role birds play in their habitat brings a greater appreciation to the art of bird watching.

This book will help you learn which habitats you should visit to find the species you are most interested in, such as warblers, thrushes, sparrows, and raptors. There are also helpful hints for making some of the more challenging bird identifications. By the time you finish this book, you will know …. So grab YOUR copy today. You'll be glad you did.

TABLE OF CONTENTS

DEDICATION

For Birda, the blue-and-gold macaw.

The loudest, most demanding, and most entertaining member of our family for the last 21 years.

ABOUT THE AUTHOR

Peter Palmieri is a retired pediatrician and the award-winning author of five novels and many published short stories. Though he is not a native of Texas, he has lived throughout the Lone Star state for over two decades – from League City to the Rio Grande Valley, from Houston to Dallas.

Peter is a bird enthusiast who likes to drive in the Texas countryside with one eye on the road, the other surveilling fence posts, and power lines. On hikes in State Parks, and even in his backyard, he's had many close encounters of the bird kind.

He is now a full-time freelance writer who contributes regularly to health and lifestyle blogs but continues writing fiction as well. He lives in the Texas Hill Country with his wife, a neurotic blue-and-gold macaw, and a couple of more or less domesticated cats.

INTRODUCTION

"No bird soars too high if he soars with his own wings."

– William Blake.

As any cowboy worth the shine on his boots is apt to remind visitors to the Lone Star state, Texas is the largest of the contiguous forty-eight. Brownville, in the southernmost corner of the state, is a whopping 785 miles from Amarillo. That's the same distance as Chicago to Philadelphia. And driving east to west, from Houston to El Paso takes some eleven hours and covers 746 miles. Consider this, El Paso is closer to San Diego, California than it is to Houston.

That's a lot of square miles, which means tons of opportunities to watch birds. From the pine forests of East Texas, through the Hill Country, along the Gulf Coast, and deep down in the Rio Grande Valley, Texas is a bird lover's haven. There are many year-round avian residents as well as seasonal visitors from Mexico and Central America.

The World Birding Center in the Rio Grande Valley attracts thousands of birding enthusiasts from all over the globe, year-round. Hiking trails and waterways throughout the state are perfect vantage points for having what I like to call, close encounters of the bird kind. And the beaches from South Padre Island to Galveston Island present still more opportunities for enjoying the rich variety of bird species in our state.

15

According to the Texas Ornithological Society, 657 bird species have been officially recorded in Texas (as of December 2021). I've picked fifty of my favorites to share with you. I chose these either because they are iconic to Texas, or because they have a particular behavior you might find shocking or endearing.

I've grouped the birds into five general categories to make our survey more manageable. Like all classification schemes, the divisions are somewhat arbitrary. The five groups are as follows: backyard birds; farms, ranches, and woodlands; rivers and waterways; the Rio Grande Valley; and the Texas Gulf Coast.

Although some birds are curious by nature, and not terribly alarmed by the presence of humans, many wild birds see us as predators. Who could blame them? Man has hunted birds for millennia, after all.

There are a few strategies that allow us to get close enough to enjoy witnessing birds in their natural habitats. First, try to be quiet. Walk softly, and whisper if you must communicate. Noise is sure to startle most birds. Remember to move slowly and smoothly. Avoid sudden jerks. If you use binoculars, raise them slowly and avoid pointing.

On outings, dress in neutral colors such as tan and khaki, as bright colors can be hostile signals for certain birds. Portable blinds are particularly useful if you plan to photograph or film. The smaller the window openings, the better. Unfortunately, these can be quite stifling during Texas summers.

Pishing can be a useful technique. It is a rudimentary call that sounds like a lisp. Basically a "psst, psst, psst." Avoid making bird calls when in the company of other birders, however. Some purists frown on the practice.

Be sure to pick your location carefully. Areas near water, whether natural or artificial, such as a fountain, or a birdbath, tend to attract birds. Feeders can be quite irresistible to many small birds . . . as well as squirrels. The advantage of feeders is that they can be fitted in your backyard, giving you a wonderful vantage point from the comfort of your own home. Be sure to change the seeds in your feeder if they are not entirely consumed within a few days.

To identify a bird, consider the size and shape first. The color of plumage can change with the seasons, but size and shape do not. When you successfully identify a bird, it may be helpful to take some written notes that you'll be able to refer to as you come across similar birds in the future.

Bird lovers keep alive a tradition that extends back to the time of cave paintings and ancient hieroglyphs. Ancient humans revered birds as godlike in many cultures. Some of the ancient folklore survives to this day. For example, owls are regarded as wise because in antiquity they were linked to the goddess Athena.

A couple of years ago, I had an experience that made me appreciate the mystical allure our ancient forefathers must have felt for the avian world. My wife and I were going for an afternoon drive on a clear day. When we drove past an empty field, something caught our eye. I immediately pulled to the side of the road.

A dark form had risen from the tall grass, flapping its large wings strenuously. It was an adult golden eagle, and from its talons trailed a thick, four-foot-long snake. It took great effort for the eagle to get airborne, the snake still curling and writhing in its clutches. The sight took our breath away. Not only for the majesty of the eagle and the snake's desperate fight for survival; the moment seemed to carry great mystical meaning – like an omen.

The sighting was the real-life acting out of the scene depicted in the middle panel of the Mexican flag: a golden eagle battling a rattlesnake while perched atop a cactus. According to legend, the leader of a nomadic tribe of the Mexican isthmus was visited in a dream by the god Huitzilopochtli and instructed to build a great city on the site where he would encounter an eagle atop a cactus, ensnaring a snake. The tribe did come across the scene and built the great pre-Columbian city of Tenochtitlan, which is now the nation's capital with the new name of Mexico City.

I watched, slack-jawed, as the eagle gained momentum and flew off, and for the first time, I not only understood the weight of the myth but felt its raw, visceral power.

Strength and majesty are just some of the admirable qualities of the avian world. But perhaps the single quality of birds that has captivated man the most is the gift of flight. Leonardo Da Vinci's sketches of birds in flight are among his most evocative. Flight, after all, symbolizes freedom. And every year, billions of birds assert their freedom by engaging in migration. In the fall, they leave their nesting sites to the north to migrate as far as South America. Many of these migratory birds will pass through the Lone Star state providing an aerial spectacle. When planning a trip to Texas, keep in mind the time of the year. Different species can be seen in different seasons. So plan accordingly.

Finally, always show respect for the environment and fellow birders. Guidelines on courteous and ethical birding are available from organizations such as the Audubon Society.

Here are a few good rules to follow:

- Do not trespass on private property
- Be sure you keep safety foremost in mind, whether you're on a rocky ridge or near a busy highway

- Be respectful of those around you – never block traffic. Don't use binoculars in residential areas (you might be mistaken for a peeping Tom!)
- When traveling to small towns, try to support the community by patronizing local businesses, such as diners and barbecue pits, rather than going to the same old mega-franchise outlets
- Whenever possible, be an ambassador for birding. Be friendly and respectful. Don't give birders a bad reputation.
- If you take a guided tour, follow the rules given by your tour guide
- Be respectful of fellow birders. Don't use flash photography or recorded bird calls. Be quiet and move slowly

And don't forget to be respectful of the birds!
- Don't flush them out from brush or undergrowth
- Don't approach or handle nests with chicks
- Don't use bird calls during mating season
- During migration season, be cognizant of the fact that some birds may be exhausted. Keep your distance so as not to stress them out unnecessarily
- If you should encounter an injured bird, place a call to a licensed wildlife rehabilitation center, and try to protect the bird from predators, pets, and traffic until help arrives

And do your small part to protect the environment. The world would be a very unhappy place indeed, without our feathered friends.
- Don't litter. Whenever you go on a birding expedition, bring a bag or sack to pack your refuse

- Stay on designated trails. This will ensure you will not trample or damage nesting sites and will help to maintain an appropriate distance between you and the creatures you want to admire.
- Don't tear down brush and trees birds may rely on
- If you are fortunate enough to own some land, plant native species of plants and place water sources such as ponds, or even small birdbaths.
- Be mindful of the environmental impact of products you use
- Support conservation groups if you have the means
- Educate friends, family members, and neighbors on bird-friendly behaviors. Who knows? They may become bird-lovers too.

Are you ready to meet some of Texas's most iconic bird species? I bet you are. Let's get started! This will be fun. And there's no need for binoculars or bird calls.

BACKYARD BIRDS

1. THE NORTHERN MOCKINGBIRD: THE STATE BIRD OF TEXAS . . . FOR NOW

Since 1927, the Northern Mockingbird has been the state bird of the Lone Star State. But if some bird enthusiasts get their way, that may change soon. The Mockingbird is a particularly cheerful, animated bird. They tend to be unafraid of people and are renowned for their vast repertoire of songs. So why kill the mockingbird?

It turns out four other states have the mockingbird as the state bird. And, if you're from Texas, that won't fly. Texans like to be different, unique. Throughout this book, we will encounter some rather singular characters for which a strong argument can be made to be named the official state bird. Perhaps, you'll find your favorite replacement for the mockingbird.

I'm actually partial to the mockingbird. Many years ago I helped rescue a chick and quickly fell in love. The mockingbird is a bright, one might say playful, creature. It bears a grey plumage with darker wings marked by shocking white feathers mid-wing. Those white flashes are a central part of their mating ritual but are used to scare up insects while hunting.

The mockingbird can be sighted throughout the state year-round. It is not uncommon to hear a young male's song as dusk approaches. It is easiest to spot them sitting atop shrubbery.

2. BAD HAIR DAY: THE TUFTED TITMOUSE

The tufted titmouse is a tiny ball of energy with a mohawk. They are among the most common backyard birds in Texas. A passerine bird in the Paridae family, the titmouse is related to the chickadee. They have tiny beaks and oversized black eyes. Their call is a repeating, "peter-peter-peter."

They typically feed on a diet of insects, spiders, and seeds, are quite fond of suet and black oil sunflower seeds. These rascals can be an annoyance to pets. They are known for plucking hair from sleeping dogs, cats, and even squirrels, to line their nests. They can be seen in most parts of the state, except the panhandle and the northernmost tip of Texas.

The tufted titmouse is a regular visitor to my back porch, where I keep an outdoor cage for my blue-and-gold macaw. They come and visit me in groups and happily clean up any seeds or flecks of fruit my macaw spills onto the floor. They'll even fly inside the cage from time to time, unintimidated by the much larger bird who lurks inside.

3. THE NORTHERN CARDINAL

For the last three years, I've had a breeding pair of cardinals living in my backyard. They make a lovely couple. Like some 90% of bird species, cardinals tend to be monogamous throughout their life. I'm happy to share my home with the cardinals, who have made it a habit to steal food from the outside cage of my blue-and-gold macaw. But there is one behavior the female exhibits which is a bit irritating.

Cardinals, like robins, tend to attack windows. They are territorial creatures. If they see their reflection in a mirror, they think it's an intruder and attack it. Repeatedly. The way to mitigate this behavior is to keep blinds down or cover the inside of the pane with paper. Unfortunately, my kitchen window does not have curtains. If I hear a repetitive tapping, I'm forced to go outside and shoo the cardinal away, lest she gets a massive headache. Interestingly, the male is more passive than the female.

Cardinals inhabit the entire state of Texas year-round. The male has a distinctive red coat, with some black plumage around its triangular beak, and sports a prominent crest. The female is terribly attractive in its brown plumage, with a black mask, and a peach beak.

4. THE BLUE JAY

A highly intelligent bird, the blue jay is a noisy mimicker of other birds. The most distinctive feature of its voice is the volume. Blue Jays are loud! This is why they are sometimes referred to as the alarm of the forest.

Blue jays will sometimes eat insects – caterpillars, beetles, and grasshoppers. But they are mostly vegetarian, preferring nuts, seeds, and acorns. It is the peculiar habit of storing acorns in the ground and forgetting to retrieve them, that makes them nature's solution to reforestation.

Blue jays can be spotted throughout Texas, except the panhandle area and the Rio Grande Valley. Males and females share the distinctive light-blue plumage with a dark collar, though the female's colors are slightly duller. Black horizontal bars can be seen extending down the tail feathers like the rungs of a ladder.

5. THE MOURNING DOVE: A UBIQUITOUS SPECIES

The mourning dove can be seen in abundance throughout the Lone Star state. Its success at proliferation is the result of its breeding habits. With only two eggs per nesting, a female dove may nest five to six times in any given year.

The mourning dove gets its name from its sad coo which, after dark, is often mistaken for the call of an owl. A high-pitched whistle can be heard as their wings flutter to take flight. They have brown plumage, with dark spots on their wings, and iridescence around the neck. Look closely and you might notice a dark smudge, the shape of a comma, on its cheeks.

In south Texas, doves will sometimes decide to make a covered outdoor ceiling fan their home. I had a beautiful specimen make a prolonged sojourn in my patio in Mission, Texas some years ago. It would fly off during the day but always return before evening. We ended up spending several weeks indoors, so as not to have to turn on that ceiling fan. When the dove finally did leave, it felt like a visiting family member had left.

6. THE MIGHTY HUMMINGBIRD

The hummingbird is the James Cagney of the avian world – compact, but tough as nails! Don't be fooled by its outward cuteness: its diminutive size, the long thin beak, the round iridescent body, its mesmerizing way of hovering and darting through the air. This little creature is extremely territorial and downright vicious.

One evening I was sitting with my wife beside a large live oak with several hummingbird feeders hanging from its boughs. Some twenty hummingbirds were hovering in that tree or perching on its branches. The birds seemed to be engaged in a cruel game. After a little contemplation, one bird would build up to courage to approach a feeder for a drink. Almost immediately, one or more of the other hummingbirds would swoop down and attack it, even though there were plenty of feeders to go around. This went on and on with no bird being able to feed in peace despite the ample supply of nectar.

If you want to attract hummingbirds to your yard, consider planting flowers rather than installing feeders of sugar water. Great choices are nasturtium, fuchsia, trailing petunias, foxgloves, and columbines. If you do use a feeder, remember that there is no reason to add dyes or food coloring.

One day, you may have the experience of coming upon a hummingbird that appears lifeless, but whose tiny heart is beating a mile a minute. The tiny creature is simply in a state of extreme exhaustion. This can be due to lack of food, or stress, such as being attacked by another bird or an outdoor cat. If this should happen, prepare a little sugar water and feed it to the hummingbird with a tiny dropper or by squeezing it from a wad of cotton. Chances are that the exhausted bird will quickly gather its strength and fly away. It will certainly make your day!

7. THE MONK PARAKEET

Wait a second. Am I really suggesting that parakeets are a backyard bird of Texas? If you live in the Dallas area, they very well could be.

I used to go jogging on the Katie Trail in Dallas, a paved biking and walking path built over what used to be a segment of The Missouri-Kansas-Texas railroad line. From time to time I would see some distinguished characters. Twice, I jogged past the former Dallas Cowboy quarterback legend, Troy Aikman (who did not wave back at me). A less intimidating visitor of the Katy Trail is the monk parakeet.

If you happen to be in Dallas, whether you're on the Katy Trail or around White Rock Lake, keep your eyes peeled for a greenish, chattery cloud. For years, a colony of some one-hundred monk parakeets has made central Dallas their home. They can be spotted on power lines in Lakewood one day, and on fence lines in Garland the next. They are not migratory birds, so they are a permanent fixture in Dallas year-round.

But parakeets are not native to Texas. This particular breed is native to South America. So how did they get there? No one knows for sure. The two theories is that the colony started with a small number of escaped pets. Others maintain a large shipment of parakeets destined for a pet shop was somehow released. Regardless of their origin, they are a sight to behold and welcome addition to the Bid D.

8. THE PAINTED BUNTING

The painted bunting is one of the most colorful visitors of Texas. It is a migratory species that typically makes its way to the Lone Star State in April and returns to its winter home in Mexico and Central America in the months of October and November. They can be spotted in most of the state except for the northern panhandle.

The male has an extravagant plumage: indigo head, russet belly, and yellow or green wings. The female is more uniformly green. Juveniles are a drab version of the female. They are frequent visitors to backyard feeders and entertain with their bright voices with a warbled phrase.

9. THE CEDAR WAXWING

The waxwing is a winter visitor to the Lone Star state. It is usually seen in parks, gardens, forest edges, and wherever fruit trees grow. Fruit, as a matter of fact, is its favorite nourishment, but it also eats insects and cedar cones. Juniper fruit, abundant in the Texas Hill Country, is one of its staples. They are known for gorging themselves on overripe fermented fruit to the point of getting drunk. When this happens, they cling to branches, fighting to maintain their balance.

The Cedar waxwing is somewhat smaller than a cardinal and has a very aerodynamic shape, with a pointed crest and a Zorro mask. The species gets its name from the waxy tips of the secondary feather. They are very sociable birds that prefer to stay with their flock and are almost never seen alone.

10. THE DICKCISSEL

The Dickcissel looks a bit like what you might get if you took a house sparrow and painted streaks on its neck and head with a yellow highlighter. It is often seen in abandoned fields and meadows, where it prefers to perch on the highest available post to sing its distinctive song. Its song, in fact, is how it got its name. It goes something like, "Dick, Dick, see, see, see." I wonder how it got its name.

11. THE TURKEY VULTURE

The Turkey Vulture, a backyard bird? No, I have not been partying with a bunch of cedar waxwings. The truth is that Turkey Vultures are a ubiquitous sight in Texas. Particularly on the side of highways where they are often seen feasting on dead deer, opossum, raccoons, porcupines, squirrels, and whatever other critter had the poor fortune of getting in the way of a motor vehicle. They are the unofficial clean-up crew in the Lone Star state, and I, for one, am glad we have them.

I have a recurring discussion with my wife. She finds buzzards in general extremely unattractive. There's something about those tiny heads that rub her the wrong way. I think vultures are quite cute. Their little eyes have a melancholy note that I find endearing. When I insist that, if she were to see vulture chicks, she'd fall in love, she makes a face that looks like she just swallowed a raw oyster.

They can be a little off-putting, with their six-foot wingspan and tiny naked red heads. And it's downright spooky when you see a flock of them perched in a single tree with their wings spread open after a rain. Scientists believe they do this to dry their wings and regulate their body temperature, but my neighbors think they do it just to creep us out. Although I appreciate their hard work, when I see them swooping in my backyard, I tend to keep my cat indoors.

12. THE HOUSE WREN

At only five inches in length, this little prankster is known for singing from dawn to dusk, making them one of the premier singers of the bird world. There is little to distinguish the male from the female. They are both tan with brown markings, with a brown bill that curves downward at its tip.

They are part of a genus known as troglodytes, which is in no way an insult. In Greek, the word simply means "cave-dweller". The wren inhabits parks, gardens, and thickets. They tend to nest in tree cavities but will sometimes make a home in an old boot or in a hanging clothespin bag.

RANCHES, FARMS, AND WOODLANDS

13. THE BROWN-HEADED COWBIRD

It's often hard to spot this member of the blackbird family, as they like to hide in bushes and shrubbery, but if you're walking by the edge of a forest, you might hear its peculiar and distinctive call. It is something of a wet gurgle that sounds like it may have been created with an electronic synthesizer.

Cowbirds are brood parasites – they don't nest. Rather, they lay their eggs in the nests of other species, most of which will incubate the eggs and raise the chicks as their own. Their name is a shortened version of the cow-pen bird, as they were often seen following cattle and bison, and taking up residence in cow pens.

The success of cowbirds of all kinds of adapting to their environment is demonstrated by the fact that they have spread so much that they are now considered somewhat of an invasive species. They encroach on and drive out other bird species. That is why they are sometimes trapped and hunted as part of conservancy efforts.

14. THE SCISSOR-TAILED FLYCATCHER

The scissor-tailed flycatcher is a truly elegant bird, whether it is perched on a fence post or sweeping through the air with its long, kite-like tail. It has a pale, creamy plumage on its head and breast, with darker wing feathers. They are commonly seen around farmhouses and in open fields but will venture into urban areas as well. They are dispersed throughout the state with the exception of the panhandle.

15. THE DOWNY WOODPECKER

The tiniest of all the woodpeckers in North America can be spotted in wooded areas throughout the state of Texas except for a corridor of land extending from the panhandle through Big Bend and down into the Rio Grande valley. Males and females have white breasts and black and white wings. The male alone has a splash of red on its head.

This resourceful bird braces itself like a tripod on the side of a tree using its stiff tail feathers. To announce his presence to mates, males will tap away on hollow logs and branches. Besides its beak, another adaptation is the woodpecker's barbed tongue which allows it to extract insects from narrow crevices.

16. BEEP! BEEP! THE GREATER ROADRUNNER

Seeing a roadrunner scurrying along the road of a country highway is a treat that always fills me with joy. And if you've ever doubted that birds are related to dinosaurs, take some time to study the predatory behavior of this spectacular bird. Roadrunners will eat anything that moves – insects, spiders, rodents, lizards, even other birds. They are fearless. If they come across a rattlesnake, they will dance around it, grab it by its neck and smash the snake's head on a rock.

How fast is a roadrunner? It has been clocked on the ground at 20 miles per hour which is not as fast as the top speed of a coyote. (It turns out you can't get all your general knowledge from cartoons.) The roadrunner has a spiky crest, a bare patch of blue and orange skin behind its bright eyes, a long supple neck, and brown tail feathers that stick up at an angle.

17. THE GREAT HORNED OWL

The largest of all owls found in Texas, the great horned owl is known for having eyes that are bigger than its stomach. Thanks to its powerful wings, it can carry away prey that weighs more than its own body weight. Rodents, skunks, raccoons, even large birds such as hawks, and the great blue heron are all on its menu. Its regal appearance, wise and unflappable, made it the perfect choice for the mascot of the Lone Star state's most prestigious institution of higher learning: Rice University.

18. THE AMERICAN ROBIN

If you happen to be in Central Texas in the springtime, keep your eyes on the sky. You may witness an annual spectacle: clouds of migrating robins. When they settle on the ground, they can blanket an entire meadow.

When a robin is happily hopping along the ground, look closely, and you may witness a peculiar behavior. As it's scratching for worms, the robin may cock its head to its side. Some people believe it does so to "listen" to the worms underground. Actually, it is focusing one eye to detect ground movement. Like those cardinals we encountered earlier, the robin will attack its reflection in a window mistaking it for another bird. Thus, demonstrating its highly territorial nature.

19. THE LOGGERHEAD SHRIKE, A FEARSOME KILLER

There is a killer on the loose in Texas. One that impales its victims on spikes. No, I'm not referring to a new installation of The Texas Chainsaw Massacre movie series. I'm talking about a tiny bird.

Were it not for its diminutive size, the loggerhead shrike would be the most frightening predator, bar none. The shrike is a songbird with the mind of a hawk., a ruthless predator of legendary aggressiveness. And if that's not enough, what the shrike does with its victims will shock you – it'll break its prey's neck with its mighty beak, and impale it on a thorn of a bush, or the spike of barbed wire. There, it will tear its victim apart to feed on it. That's why in Texas this little menace is known as the Butcher Bird.

Fortunately, the shrike is only nine inches long and light enough to perch on a reed. He hunts insects, frogs, small mammals, lizards, and even small birds. He resembles the mockingbird, in some respects, but has a sharp, down-turned beak for tearing at its prey.

41

20. THE SAVANNAH SPARROW

The savannah sparrow is an occasional victim of the loggerhead shrike, which we've just come to know and fear. Like all sparrows, it is part of a family of passerines called emberizine which, for the most part, inhabits North and South America. The most abundant winter sparrow in Texas, it can be found in grasslands, pastures, and other open habitats, but can be commonly seen on fences and roadsides.

Its upper part is streaked brown and white. It has a white belly and a short, notched tail. Its legs are long in relation to its body and have a pinkish hue.

21. THE BARN SWALLOW

Austin, Texas is renowned for being the home to a large colony of Mexican bats that roost inside the Congress Avenue bridge. Each night, millions of bats swoop out from their lair deep in the bridge and eat 10,000 to 20,000 pounds of flying insects, including the dreaded mosquito. But the Mexican bat is not the only mosquito exterminator in the Lone Star state. The barn swallow does its part in reducing the population of pesky mosquitoes and keeping Texans more or less comfortable.

The barn swallow is a fixture in Texas skies in hot summer evenings. But when winter comes, they prefer to sojourn in warmer climates, well south of the border. Seven inches in length, with dark blue to black upperparts and a cinnamon belly, and slender, forked tails, this swallow will glide low over the surface of the water and drink mid-flight. It gets its name for its propensity to build mud nests on the sides of barns, but houses and the underside of bridges are not off-limits.

I have a permanent memory of a house swallow on an outdoor wall of my house. While the home was in construction, a swallow decided to make a nest there. As construction finished and we moved into the house, the swallow moved to a more sensible location. I tried cleaning the abandoned mud home from my wall with a power washer. No matter how hard I tried, and which angle I directed the water stream, a thin ghost of mud remained. I figure it's there for good, and I don't mind. It's become a permanent reminder of yet another friendly visitor to our home.

22. THE NORTHERN HARRIER

A few days ago, I went on a leisurely bike ride with my wife. It was late in the afternoon and the sky had just started to darken, when off to my left, behind a chain-linked fence, atop a four-by-four wooden post I spotted a beautiful bird of prey: a northern harrier. I stopped and spent a few minutes chatting with it, until he lost interest in the conversation and flew away.

Northern harriers resemble red-tailed hawks but are slimmer and have a rather small beak. Old-timers sometimes call them marsh hawks, for their propensity of hunting over wet, boggy fields. They are low-flying predators, gliding just above the ground in search of their next meal.

23. THE WESTERN KINGBIRD

If you're driving down a country road in Texas and see a bird with an olive-colored head, a gray breast, and a yellow belly sitting on a fence post, you may be face to face with a western kingbird. And don't get the wrong impression – the bird is not slacking off sitting on that post. The western kingbird is no slouch. It is on the lookout for grasshoppers, crickets, and other critters to hunt. To help their offspring learn how to hunt, parents will bring wounded but still living insects back to their nests and let the young ones finish them off.

24. THE SUMMER TANAGER

There are quite a few species people generally refer to as "red birds". But if ever you should see a red birdy in the company of a green birdy, you can be quite sure they are a mating pair of summer tanagers. The male summer tanager is not quite as brilliantly crimson as its near relative, the scarlet tanager, but is still a sight to behold.

25. THE WILD TURKEY

The wild turkey is the largest native game bird of Texas. Though the population of turkeys suffered a major decline in the early 1900s, the species has made a remarkable comeback and now inhabits most of the Lone Star state. Though the male turkey (known as a tom) is typically seen trudging on the ground with a harem of up to twenty females, he is an impressively strong and nimble flyer. At night, turkeys roost in trees to avoid predators such as coyotes.

A large flock of wild turkeys sometimes crosses my backyard to access the ranch behind our property. My cats know to stay away from them. They will not be intimidated. Not even by me, when I happen to step outside and come face to face with them.

It is sometimes said that Benjamin Franklin had proposed the wild turkey as the national symbol. Historians believe the story is apocryphal but it is not without foundation. Franklin thought the turkey "a bird of courage that would not hesitate to attach a grenadier of the British Guards who should presume to invade his farm yard with a red coat on." The eagle, in the founding father's estimation, was "a rank coward."

In view of the fact that Americans celebrate several holidays by cooking a turkey, it is just as well that the bald eagle became our nation's symbol.

26. THE CHIHUAHUAN RAVEN

It turns out not everything is bigger in Texas. The Chihuahuan Raven is slightly smaller than the common raven but is every bit as smart and mischievous. It has a raspier, throatier call than its cousin, the common crow, and in-flight can be seen to have a tighter, wedge-lie tail compared to the crow's fan-like rump.

Male ravens will perform a barnstorming aerial show to attract a mate. They will fly high, then tumble down as if out of control before righting themselves again. When they do find a mate, they will often use the same nest repeatedly for several seasons.

RIVERS AND WATERWAYS

27. THE DOUBLE-CRESTED CORMORANT

Landa Park is a natural refuge just beyond downtown New Braunfels, north of San Antonio. The Comal River springs from two crevices in the limestone, fed by Edward's Aquifer. In between the two rivulets, there is a small peninsula of land, shaded by stately Bald Cypresses, and at its tip, where the streams come together and the river widens, there is a large wooden gazebo.

If you sit here by the water's edge on a late afternoon, there is a high likelihood that you will be able to witness a talented fisher, the double-crested cormorant. This large black bird, with a long, supple neck, will float on the water's surface and intermittently dive, disappearing into the water below. It will resurface with a small fish in its hooked bill, swallow it with a few jutting spasms of the neck, seem to lose interest for a short while, and dive again.

If it decides to fly in search of a better fishing spot, it will take some time to clear the water's surface, then glide gracefully, skimming the surface of the river. Cormorants can sometimes be seen on the stump of a tree drying their wings. Surprisingly for a water bird, its outer feathers are not waterproof. It turns out this is a special adaptation for dive fishing as the wettable feathers decrease buoyancy and reduce drag.

28. THE CANVASBACK

This is a tan duck with a black bill and a sloping forehead. They inhabit reservoirs, ponds, and rivers throughout the Lone Star state. The females are philopatric, that is, they return to nest at their birthplace. The males, on the other hand, will drift to new digs. This means both males and females will have a new mate each year, ensuring differentiation in the genetic makeup of the progeny.

29. THE SNOWY EGRET

Graceful and impeccably coiffed, the all-white snowy egret has a wingspan of over three feet. It can be seen wading in shallow waterways in isolation but may join large colonies to nest. The eggs of the snowy egret hatch asynchronously, one egg at a time separated by a few days. Sadly, the last of the three to five chicks to hatch will die of starvation.

30. THE LITTLE BLUE HERON

The Little Blue Heron is similar in shape and size to the snowy egret has a juvenile, but then trades its ivory white plumage for one that is slate gray to blue. This darker coloration makes them less conspicuous in marshy vegetation. It tends to hunt alone, or in the company of egrets. The little blue heron is a methodical hunter. It lumbers slowly and deliberately as it stalks its prey.

31. THE BELTED KINGFISHER

My first close and personal experience with a belted Kingfisher happened some twenty years ago at the Santa Ana National Wildlife Refuge, just south of the city of McAllen. The Santa Ana refuge straddles several sweeping curves of the Rio Grande River, on the border with Mexico. It is a serene park with a tidy visitor's area featuring its own bookstore.

That day was so hot, not even the air felt like moving. There were few visitors, so my family and I had the park largely to ourselves. It was when we climbed on a wooden outlook terrace facing a marsh that we saw him perched on a wooden post. I expect he spotted us too but was apparently too preoccupied with his self-preening to pay us much heed.

The belted kingfisher is one of the most recognizable birds seen by water's edge thanks to its distinctively large head marked by a ruffled crest and a large straight beak. It takes practice to be a good fisher. That's why adult kingfishers will drop dead fish in the water and have their young retrieve them so they can learn the ropes. If you happen to see a kingfisher regurgitate something, that's not a hairball. It's a bone pellet. Kingfishers are unable to pass fish bones through their digestive tracts.

32. THE PURPLE GALLINULE

The purple gallinule may be one of the most colorful birds in Texas. It has a rich indigo breast, green upper parts, and a scarlet beak with a yellow tip. One might think this bird has an identity crisis. The author Gary Clark has noted that it "swims like a duck, wades like a heron, and perches on reeds like a bittern." Its super-long toes allow it to walk atop floating vegetation as it hunts for food.

33. THE AMERICAN COOT

Do not mistake this waterfowl for a duck. Check its feet. You'll notice that whereas a duck has webbed feet, the coot has lobed toes that are not interconnected. This gray bird has a white bill that slopes downward at a rather acute angle. Since it has short wings, it needs quite a long runway to achieve lift-off.

THE RIO GRANDE VALLEY

34. THE CHACHALACA

If you ever have the good fortune of visiting the Rio Grande Valley, you might feel as though this southernmost region of Texas is a country of its own. It has an exotic feel, with a warm familiarity. And it is one of the best birdwatching areas in the entire country.

One curious and exotic species you might encounter is the chachalaca, sometimes known as the Mexican pheasant. If you hear its call, you will immediately know how it got its name. This dark gray bird may hide in brush, under mesquites, or swoop down from the branch of an oak. In some countries in central and south America, the chachalaca is considered good eating. This is contributing to a marked reduction in its number south of the border.

In cities like McAllen, Texas, the chachalaca is a backyard intruder that is not impeded by tall wooden fences. Small flocks will move out from under brush and mesquite and sail to the lower branches of an oak. From there, they will glide into a yard searching for food while cackling among each other in their distinctive way.

35. THE WHITE WINGED DOVE

There is perhaps no bird more iconic to the Rio Grande Valley than the white-winged dove. It is slightly larger than the mourning dove and has a prominent rim of white feathers on the forward edge of its wings. A consumer of fruits and seeds, it will make escapades to feeders from time to time. Otherwise, it will loiter in a patch of shrubbery.

36. THE CRESTED CARACARA

If a bird has a strange name, it is probably an inhabitant of the Rio Grande Valley. The caracara is a member of the falcon family. Its head has a black cap and a curved beak, red at this base, which gives it an almost vulture-like appearance. It is an avid hunter but will settle for carrion it might encounter on the rural fields it calls home.

37. ANHINGA ANHINGA

Also known as the snakebird (for its penchant for swimming with only its head exposed) and the water turkey, this creature resembles a cormorant in body shape and size, but its beak is long and straight rather than hooked at the end. Its scientific name comes from the Tupi Indians of Brazil. Like the crested cormorant, after a good swim, the anhinga will need to seek out a perch to spread its wings and allow its feathers to dry.

38. THE TROPICAL PARULA

You are only likely to find this tiny warbler in the Rio Grande Valley, from McAllen to Harlingen. It lives in areas where Spanish moss is plentiful. The throat and breast are the color of a ripe mango. The upperparts are dark gray. Two streaks of white are painted on each wing.

39. THE PYRRHULOXIA

This slate gray bird resembles a cardinal in body shape, though it has a smaller, squat beak. It is shyer than the cardinal. The best time to spot one is in the early morning. The male is a true gentleman. He feeds the female during courtship and when she is busy incubating her eggs.

40. THE BLACK PHOEBE

This is a squat, round bird, some seven inches in length. It is entirely charcoal in color, except for a patch of white on its belly. The male performs an elaborate mating ritual, singing mid-flight, descending slowly as it tries to catch a female's eye. When perched on a branch, it can be recognized by a bobbing or pumping of its tail.

41. THE BLACK-HEADED GROSBEAK

Grosbeaks are smaller cousins of cardinals. The black-headed grosbeak, as its name implies, has a black head and black wings with white blotches. Its breast and belly are mustard yellow. Every year, this tiny bird enjoys a buffet of migrating Monarch butterflies, being immune to the insect's toxic effect that it has on other predators.

42. THE GREAT KISKADEE

Like the anhinga, the kiskadee gets its name from the Tupi Indians of Brazil. It is an attractive flycatcher, with rusty wings, a yellow breast, and a white head featuring a black mask running horizontally over its eyes. It lives near water where it will feed on tadpoles, small frogs, and minnows.

43. THE FERRUGINOUS PYGMY OWL

Ferruginous simply means rusty, which is an apt description for the color of this owl's plumage. Unlike most owls, which are nocturnal predators, the ferruginous pygmy owl prefers to hunt by the light of day, which makes it easier for birdwatchers to spot. Standing only six inches, it's quite small, but it bears a ferocious appearance thanks to its bright yellow eyes.

44. THE GREAT-TAILED GRACKLE

On warm evenings in urban areas such as McAllen, the air is filled by a chorus of screeching and cawing so loud one has to speak up to make themselves heard. The background noise is provided by grackles, huddled in the trees of grocery store parking lots, and lining power lines along highways. The grackles have a shiny, black plumage with glints of blue. It is a rather insistent panhandler, hopping up to humans in hopes of a handful of bread, a few nachos, or a piece of hamburger. In the wild, it will feed on insects, grain, seeds, small critters, and the eggs of other birds.

THE TEXAS GULF COAST

45. THE BLACK-BELLIED PLOVER

The black-bellied plover can be seen scampering across beaches from South Padre Island to Galveston, unperturbed by sun-bathers and beachcombers. The males have a distinctive black plumage running down from their necks to their belly, with marbled gray wings and dorsum. The female is entirely tan and gray. They dart across the sands, near the gulf waters, to hunt insects that compose the entirety of their diet.

46. THE SANDERLING

Another beachcomber, the sanderling has longer legs than the plover, a gray dorsum with rusty spots, and a completely white breast and belly. They can be seen dashing back and forth with the movement of the waves trying to get their fill of insects. As it rollicks in the waves, one would never guess that this small bird nests in the Arctic and can winter anywhere from North America to the southern tip of Argentina.

47. THE ROSEATE SPOONBILL

The roseate spoonbill has a bit of an awkward, even comical appearance. Known also as the "flame bird" and "banjo bill" the spoonbill's body shape and color resemble that of a flamingo, but it is actually in the ibis family. To feed, it uses its large bill to scoop up briny water and sift small sea creatures.

48. THE BLACK NECKED STILT

As its name implies, the black necked stilt has legs that seem far too long for the size of its body. It also has a trim long beak ideal for feeding on aquatic insects. The Gulf Coast of Texas is known for temperatures that frequently exceed 100 degrees Fahrenheit in the summer. To keep her eggs cool, a black necked stilt will waterlog its belly feather and bathe its eggs.

49. THE AMERICAN AVOCET

Avocets are long-legged shorebirds with webbed feet and a curious up-turned long beak. It prefers shallow brackish water where it feeds on insects, aquatic plants, and small crustaceans. The upturned bill is the perfect tool to stir up mud and send insects scurrying.

50. THE BLACK SKIMMER

From a distance, the black skimmer appears not to have eyes. In truth, they are so dark they are hidden by the black pirate cape on this predator's head. The black head feathers extend down the back of the neck and cover most of the body, except for the neck and breast with are snowy white. The highly specialized beak of the skimmer is two-toned – red at the base and black at the tip – and has a peculiar design. The lower bill is longer than the upper.

Black skimmers will fly in numbers, just above the water's edge, their razor-sharp jaws skimming the water for fish. It feasts on small fish, such as minnows. Onshore, the skimmer appears less agile due to its short, rather stubby legs. Nonetheless, they will fiercely defend their nests from intruders.

OTHER HELPFUL RESOURCES

The World Birding Center of the Rio Grande Valley: one of the most important bird-lover destination in Texas http://www.theworldbirdingcenter.com/

Texas Ornithological Society: a comprehensive source of information on Texas birds https://texasbirds.org/

Texas State List: the list of official Texas bird species: https://www.texasbirdrecordscommittee.org/texas-state-list

Audubon Guide to North American Birds: A great resource from the premier bird advocacy group, the Audubon Society. https://www.audubon.org/bird-guide

The Cornell lab of Ornithology: This is an excellent resource for all things birds from Cornell University. Their app can help identify birds sounds. https://www.birds.cornell.edu/ eBird https://ebird.org/home An online database of bird observations providing scientists, researchers and amateur naturalists with real-time data about bird distribution and abundance.

U.S. Fish and Wildlife Services Birds of Conservation Concern https://www.fws.gov/birds/management/managed-species/birds-of-conservation-concern.php

The National Audubon Society. The National Audubon Society protects birds and the places they need, today and tomorrow, throughout the Americas using science, advocacy, education, and on-the-ground conservation. https://www.audubon.org/

Bird Collisions

To prevent bird collisions with windows, place your feeders more than 30 feet from a window or less than three feet from the window. 30 feet away from a window is a safe distance to prevent collisions caused by reflections wile 3 feet prevents birds from building up the momentum while flying to cause a fatal collision

IMAGE RESOURCES

1. By Rhododendrites - Own work, CC BY-SA 4.0, https://commons.wikimedia.org/w/index.php?curid=99104839

2. By Basar - Own work, CC BY-SA 3.0, https://commons.wikimedia.org/w/index.php?curid=32290304

3. By Rhododendrites - Own work, CC BY-SA 4.0, https://commons.wikimedia.org/w/index.php?curid=100287792

4. By Rhododendrites - Own work, CC BY-SA 4.0, https://commons.wikimedia.org/w/index.php?curid=103770921

5. By http://www.naturespicsonline.com/ - http://www.naturespicsonline.com/galleries/Nature15/_mg_8449a.htm, CC BY-SA 2.5, https://commons.wikimedia.org/w/index.php?curid=1083262

6. By Joseph C Boone - Own work, CC BY-SA 4.0, https://commons.wikimedia.org/w/index.php?curid=71169567

7. By Bernard DUPONT from FRANCE - Monk Parakeet (Myiopsitta monachus), CC BY-SA 2.0, https://commons.wikimedia.org/w/index.php?curid=50340187

8. By Doug Janson - Own work, CC BY-SA 3.0, https://commons.wikimedia.org/w/index.php?curid=6490569

9. By Judy Gallagher - Cedar Waxwing - Bombycilla cedrorum, George Washington's Birthplace National Monument, Colonial Beach, Virginia, CC BY 2.0, https://commons.wikimedia.org/w/index.php?curid=66899682

10. https://en.wikipedia.org/wiki/Dickcissel#/media/File:DickcisselA.jpg

11. By Peter K Burian - Own work, CC BY-SA 4.0,
    https://commons.wikimedia.org/w/index.php?curid=63275220

12. By S. King, US NPS - [1] at US NPS, Public Domain,
    https://commons.wikimedia.org/w/index.php?curid=8156486

13. By Rhododendrites - Own work, CC BY-SA 4.0,
    https://commons.wikimedia.org/w/index.php?curid=105354857

14. By Kramer, Gary - U.S. Fish and Wildlife Service, Public Domain,
    https://commons.wikimedia.org/w/index.php?curid=7972225

15. By Wolfgang Wander - self-made /
    http://www.pbase.com/wwcsig/image/77075634, CC BY-SA 3.0,
    https://commons.wikimedia.org/w/index.php?curid=3112981

16. By drumguy8800 (xvisionx.com) - Own work, CC BY-SA 3.0,
    https://commons.wikimedia.org/w/index.php?curid=1332253

17. By Greg Hume - Own work, CC BY-SA 3.0,
    https://commons.wikimedia.org/w/index.php?curid=28866977

18. By en:User:Mdf - Own work, CC BY-SA 3.0,
    https://commons.wikimedia.org/w/index.php?curid=253938

19. By Lanius_ludovicianus_-Texas_-USA-8.jpg: Terry
    Rossderivative work: Snowmanradio (talk) - originally posted to
    Flickr as "Whoa dude!" and uploaded to commons as
    Lanius_ludovicianus_-Texas_-USA-8.jpg, CC BY-SA 2.0,
    https://commons.wikimedia.org/w/index.php?curid=8687072

20. By Cephas - Own work, CC BY-SA 3.0,
    https://commons.wikimedia.org/w/index.php?curid=6785567

21. By I, Malene, CC BY 2.5,
    https://commons.wikimedia.org/w/index.php?curid=20612

22. By Len Blumin from Mill Valley, California, United States - Northern Harrier, CC BY 2.0, https://commons.wikimedia.org/w/index.php?curid=5001379

23. By MdFderivative work: Berichard (talk) - Tyrannus-verticalis-001.jpg, CC BY-SA 3.0, https://commons.wikimedia.org/w/index.php?curid=9041568

24. By Gonzalo Zepeda Martínez - https://www.inaturalist.org/photos/2906701?size=original, CC BY-SA 4.0, https://commons.wikimedia.org/w/index.php?curid=110961275

25. By Riki7 - Own work, Public Domain, https://commons.wikimedia.org/w/index.php?curid=6957499

26. By Quinn Dombrowski from Chicago, USA - Day 179: I'm Addicted To Your Spirit, RavenUploaded by Snowmanradio, CC BY-SA 2.0, https://commons.wikimedia.org/w/index.php?curid=15716648

27. By Mdf - English Wikipedia (deleted since), CC BY-SA 3.0, https://commons.wikimedia.org/w/index.php?curid=327095

28. By Frank Schulenburg - Own work, CC BY-SA 3.0, https://commons.wikimedia.org/w/index.php?curid=30718759

29. By © Frank Schulenburg, CC BY-SA 3.0, https://commons.wikimedia.org/w/index.php?curid=30717494

30. By Dario Sanches from São Paulo, Brazil - GARÇA-AZUL (Egretta caerulea)Uploaded by Snowmanradio, CC BY-SA 2.0, https://commons.wikimedia.org/w/index.php?curid=12106836

31. By "Mike" Michael L. Baird, CC BY 2.0, https://commons.wikimedia.org/w/index.php?curid=1874159

32. By http://www.birdphotos.com - Own work, CC BY 3.0, https://commons.wikimedia.org/w/index.php?curid=4485528

33. By Casey Klebba - Own work, CC BY-SA 4.0, https://commons.wikimedia.org/w/index.php?curid=72255655

34. By Fernando Flores, CC BY-SA 2.0, https://commons.wikimedia.org/w/index.php?curid=44435275

35. By SearchNet Media - White-Winged DovesUploaded by Snowmanradio, CC BY 2.0, https://commons.wikimedia.org/w/index.php?curid=7339700

36. By Andreas Trepte - Own work, CC BY-SA 4.0, https://commons.wikimedia.org/w/index.php?curid=43914003

37. By Tim from Ithaca - Anhinga, CC BY 2.0, https://commons.wikimedia.org/w/index.php?curid=15526948

38. By Dario Sanches from São Paulo, Brazil - MARIQUITA (Parula pitiayumi)Uploaded by snowmanradio, CC BY-SA 2.0, https://commons.wikimedia.org/w/index.php?curid=16502590

39. By Andy Morffew, CC BY 2.0, https://commons.wikimedia.org/w/index.php?curid=110960640

40. By Pranav Tadepalli - Own work, CC BY-SA 4.0, https://commons.wikimedia.org/w/index.php?curid=101786336

41. By Alan Vernon - Male Black headed grosbeak (Pheucticus melanocephalus)Uploaded by Snowmanradio, CC BY 2.0, https://commons.wikimedia.org/w/index.php?curid=12140735

42. By Mike & Chris - Great KIskadeeUploaded by berichard, CC BY-SA 2.0, https://commons.wikimedia.org/w/index.php?curid=15574732

43. By User: Sky Jacobs - Own work, CC BY-SA 3.0,
https://commons.wikimedia.org/w/index.php?curid=2666209

44. By Patrick Coin (Patrick Coin) - Photograph taken by Patrick Coin, CC BY-SA 2.5,
https://commons.wikimedia.org/w/index.php?curid=1528397

45. By © Hans Hillewaert, CC BY-SA 3.0,
https://commons.wikimedia.org/w/index.php?curid=15256156

46. By JJ Harrison (https://www.jjharrison.com.au/) - Own work, CC BY-SA 3.0,
https://commons.wikimedia.org/w/index.php?curid=13336542

47. By Jgocfoto - Own work, CC BY-SA 4.0,
https://commons.wikimedia.org/w/index.php?curid=100059430

48. By © Frank Schulenburg, CC BY-SA 3.0,
https://commons.wikimedia.org/w/index.php?curid=29091464

49. By Dan Pancamo - originally posted to Flickr as Quintana June 2nd 2010, CC BY-SA 2.0,
https://commons.wikimedia.org/w/index.php?curid=12182228

50. By Andreas Trepte - Own work, CC BY-SA 4.0,
https://commons.wikimedia.org/w/index.php?curid=43432734

READ OTHER
50 THINGS TO KNOW ABOUT BIRDS IN THE
UNITED STATES BOOKS

50 Things to Know About Birds in Illinois

50 Things to Know About Birds in Missouri

50 Things to Know About Birds in New York

50 Things to Know About Birds in Oklahoma

50 Things to Know About Birds in Oregon

50 Things to Know About Birds in Pennsylvania

50 Things to Know

Stay up to date with new releases on Amazon:

https://amzn.to/2VPNGr7

CZYKPublishing.com

50 Things to Know

We'd love to hear what you think about our content! Please leave your honest review of this book on Amazon and Goodreads. We appreciate your positive and constructive feedback. Thank you.